CAT ALPHABET

Words by Robin Feiner

A is for **A**byssinian.
Aside from having the most 'awww'-inspiring eyes and the perkiest ears you'll ever see, this regal, legendary breed is also known for being able to learn a few tricks. Sit. Paw. Lie down. But watch out! These 'Clowns of the Cat Kingdom' would love to pull a few tricks on you.

Bb

B is for **B**ritish Shorthair. Once bred only to be blue, these legends now come in a variety of colors. White, black, red, cream, or chocolate—take your pick—they're all adorable with their teddy bear faces. And this feline friend is arguably the most loyal cat that's ever existed.

C is for Chinchilla. Sometimes all you need is a gigantic ball of fur. And that's exactly what you'll get with the legendary Chinchilla. They're hefty, fantastic to pet, and enthrall you with their stunning lime-green eyes. Just make sure you never bring your white Chinchilla out in the snow, or you might lose them.

D is for Devon Rex.
With a minuscule face and ears as large as parachutes, the 'Alien Cat' is as mischievous and playful as they come. With an attitude as fun and quirky as its looks, the Devon Rex will adopt its humans and remain their faithful companion.

E is for Egyptian Mau.
One of the purest and
oldest breeds known to man,
this legend is renowned for
its ability to breed without
assistance from humans.
Their lineage dates back
more than 3,000 years to
Africa. Maus are also known
for being one of the most
independent cat breeds.

Ff

F is for Scottish Fold.
Earning its name, thanks
to its distinctive folded ears,
the Scottish Fold also has a
unique purr. It's as if they
know just how to speak with
their humans. To top it all
off, they are as sweet as the
looks on their adorable faces!
Awww!

G is for German Rex. Truly a legend, this cat's one of the rarest breeds in the entire world. If its over-sized ears, large eyes, and small face don't win you over, then its playfulness, intelligence, and loyalty will. The German Rex is one of the few cats patient enough to be trained and loves playing fetch.

H is for Himalayan.
The legendary blue-eyed
'Himmie' takes its name from
its striking black and white
colors, resembling the famed
rabbits and mountain goats
populating the Himalayan
Mountains. But unlike mountain
goats, this playful breed is
much more at home scaling
the heights of the living
room sofa.

I is for 'Isle of Man' Manx. Nicknamed 'Rumpy' or 'Stumpy,' these round-bodied, short-tailed beauties originated on the Isle of Man between England and Ireland. A Manx is a loving and playful companion, eager to learn new tricks. These little Einsteins will prowl the house, opening doors and turning on faucets.

J is for **J**apanese Bobtail. Buddhist monks first domesticated this short and fluffy-tailed cat way back in the 1600s, and the Bobtails proved themselves excellent mousers on the ancient Silk Road. These little guys love to chat with their humans with voices so musical, they sound like they're singing!

K is for **K**orat.
One of Thailand's 'good luck' cats, the Korat sports a gorgeous silver-tipped coat and is covered in hearts! It has a heart-shaped face and nose, another heart on top of its head, and a heart shape on its chest. But some people say its greatest heart is the one inside this lovable creature.

L is for LaPerm.
They might look like they were just shocked by electricity, but that's simply part of the appeal with the lovable and legendary LaPerm! For this breed, there's no better place to nap than directly in their owner's lap. So get ready for an extra bout of snuggling.

M is for Maine Coon.
While some have speculated
that the Maine Coon is part
raccoon and part cat, those
theories are pure myth.
What truly separates these
legendary 'Gentle Giants'
from their peers is the sheer
size to which they can grow.
Is it a cat—or a lion? Who
cares? It's stunning either way.

N is for **N**orwegian Forest. As one of the rarest breeds in the world, this legendary fluffball is all fur and no fuss. They're known for being friendly, calm, and incredibly intelligent. And with all their magnificent white, gray, and auburn hair, the Norwegian Forest is a perfect cat to scoop up and smother with love.

O is for Oriental Shorthair. Like a Sphynx, but with hair! With comically large ears— think Chihuahua ears on a cat—and a super sleek physique, this cat rules the room. 'Ornamentals' will follow you like your shadow, using their honking voices to ask about your day and tell you all about theirs.

P is for Persian.
A short face, chubby nose, and a tiny body that you just want to squish—those are the features that make this cat the stuff of legends. Persians might be hard to tame, as they're known for their independence. Neither climbers nor jumpers, Persians are content with striking photogenic poses all day.

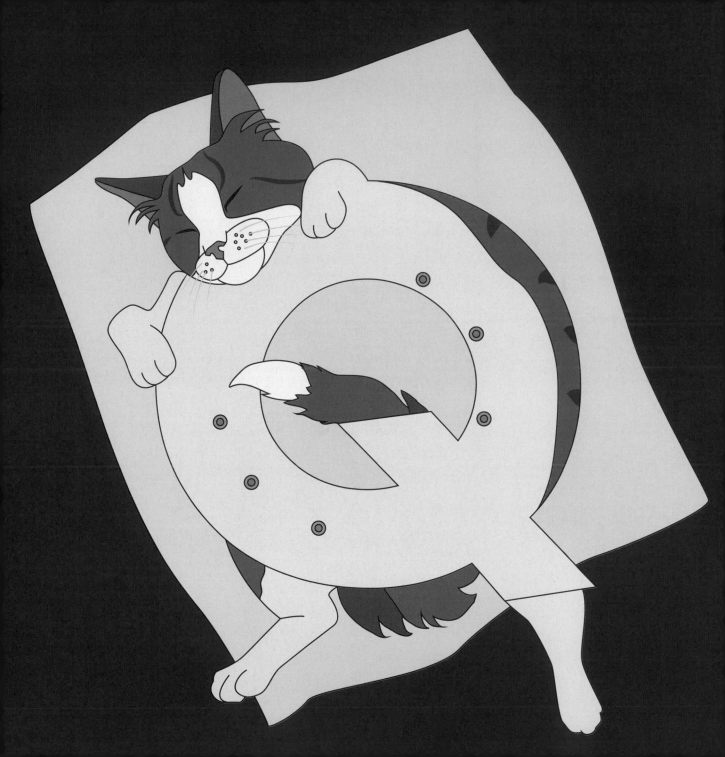

Qq

Q is for **Q**ueen Cat.
Here's a fun fact about our feline friends: female cats capable of breeding are referred to as 'queens' in cat lingo. After a queen has given birth to a litter, she is then referred to as a 'dam'—meaning she is now a mother. Absolute purr-fection!

R is for **R**agdoll.
Most cats don't want you
to come anywhere near them
for cuddle time—but not this
legendary breed. Cozy up
to them, plop them in your
loving arms and stare into
their beautiful blue eyes.
Chances are they'll go limp
and stare happily back
at you—just like a ragdoll.

S is for Siamese.
Is there a more legendary cat than the Siamese? It's believed they've been around since the 14th century, making them one of the oldest modern breeds in history. They were even given royal treatment in Thailand hundreds of years ago because of their uniquely colored coats.

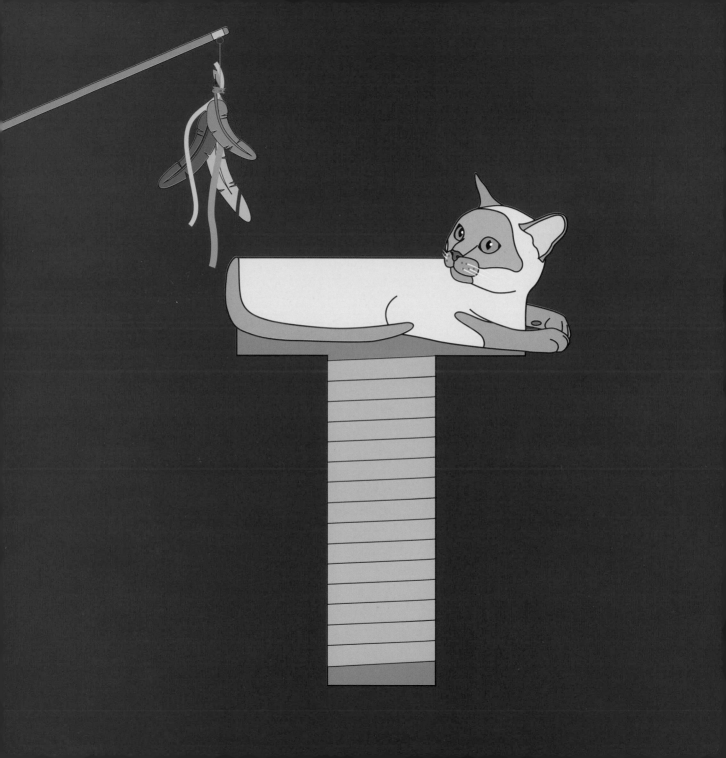

T is for Tonkinese. This well-mannered feline legend is the result of cross-breeding two of the most well-known cats known to man: the Burmese and Siamese. Their piercing blue eyes shine like the vibrant Caribbean Sea, and they're famous for meowing more like quacky ducks than purring cats.

U is for Ukrainian Levkoy. There might be no breed of cat that is more unique than this shorthaired Ukrainian legend. Stunning aqua-blue colored eyes? Check. Minuscule, folded ears? Check. Wrinkly heads that make them look 100 years old? Check, check, and check!

V is for Turkish Vankedisi. Most cats will sprint away at the first sight of water. They don't like swimming or even going for a short dip. But these legendary Turkish furbabies have proven to be a wonderful exception. With their long, winding orange tails, the Vankedisi will bounce right into any body of water!

W is for American **W**irehair. With a coat of fur that looks like a fuzzy wool blanket, the Wirehair has quickly become a favorite member of American families. They're emotionally intelligent, and they'll often link their emotions with those of their owner. If you're sad, they're sad—but if you're happy, so are they!

X is for **Ex**otic Shorthair. The 'Lazy Man's Persian Cat' shares a lot in common with the famed Persian breed, most of all their plump, adorable faces. But while Persians are notoriously high-maintenance, Exotics are the type to sit back all day and relax. In other words, they're the perfect couch buddy.

Y is for York Chocolate. For a while, the Chocolate was the rarest cat on the entire planet. Aside from being incredibly fluffy and darker than the night, York Chocolates were known for their superior levels of intelligence and loyalty. Sadly, the breed is now extinct—truly making them the stuff of legend.

Z is for Brazilian Shorthair. This legendary Brazilian breed has one of the most beautiful coats of fur you'll ever lay eyes on. Quite large and muscular, they can grow to be among the biggest breeds of house cats around. No surprise then that they're also known for being incredibly cocky!

The ever-expanding legendary library

EXPLORE THESE LEGENDARY ALPHABETS & MORE AT WWW.ALPHABETLEGENDS.COM

CAT ALPHABET
www.alphabetlegends.com

Published by Alphabet Legends Pty Ltd in 2022
Created by Beck Feiner
Copyright © Alphabet Legends Pty Ltd 2022

Printed and bound in China.

9780645487053

ALPHABET LEGENDS